the **information** store
☎ 01603 773114
email: tis@ccn.ac.uk

21 DAY LOAN ITEM

A FINE WILL BE CHARGED ON OVERDUE ITEMS

Hodder & Stoughton

A MEMBER OF THE HODDER HEADLINE GROUP

Acknowledgements
Photos: pp. 3, 6, 9, 12, 16, 26 © Colorsport.
pp. 20, 23 © Action Images.
Cover photo: © Action Images.

Orders: please contact Bookpoint Ltd, 39 Milton Park, Abingdon, Oxon OX14 4TD. Telephone: (44) 01235 400414, Fax: (44) 01235 400454. Lines are open from 9.00–6.00, Monday to Saturday, with a 24 hour message answering service. Email address: orders@bookpoint.co.uk

British Library Cataloguing in Publication Data
A catalogue record for this title is available from The British Library

ISBN 0 340 701048

First published 1997
Impression number 10 9 8 7 6 5 4 3 2
Year 2004 2003 2002 2001 2000 1999 1998

Typeset by Fakenham Photosetting Ltd, Fakenham, Norfolk.
Printed in Great Britain for Hodder & Stoughton Educational, a division of Hodder Headline Plc, 338 Euston Road, London NW1 3BH by Page Bros, Norwich.

Contents

1 The Spurs

Glory, glory Tottenham Hotspur
Glory, glory Tottenham Hotspur
Glory, glory Tottenham Hotspur
And the Spurs go marching on!

That's Spurs' song!
Other fans have sung it,
but it's still Spurs' song.

And it's right,
because Spurs have always been
the 'Glory, glory' team.

Other teams believe in hard work
and playing for the team.
Spurs believe in style and stars.

Other teams believe in winning at all cost.
Spurs believe in thrilling the fans.

Other teams have won the League more,
and scored more points.
But Spurs have won the Cup more,
and scored more goals.

And what great goals they have scored!
The sort of goals you never forget.
The sort of goals
old men tell their grandchildren about.
The sort of goals
you see again and again on television.

Mind you, they've let in a few too!

Glory, glory!
Gascoigne scores for Spurs.
Semi-final FA Cup, 1991.

2 The early years

Why Tottenham **Hotspur**?
Tottenham is a part of London,
like Chelsea or West Ham.
But why Hotspur?
Why not 'City', or 'United'?

The men who founded the club,
over 100 years ago,
liked history.
Their hero was Harry Hotspur.
He was a famous fighter in the Middle Ages.
But he wasn't famous just for his fighting,
he was famous for his style
and good looks as well.
So Spurs took their name from him,
and also their style.

They played on a field behind a local pub.
The pub owned the field,
but the landlord didn't mind.
He thought it would be good for business.
The pub was called The White Hart,
and the little path going down to the field
was called White Hart Lane.

The pub is still there,
but behind it now is the grandest,
and most expensive ground in England.
This is White Hart Lane,
the home of Spurs.

There's one other story
from the early days of Spurs.
In 1909, they went on a tour of South America.
They brought back a parrot.
It became Spurs' mascot.
Every time they won,
it cawed and flapped its wings.
Every time they lost,
it moped, and looked sick.
In 1919, Spurs were relegated.
The parrot died!

And that's how 'sick as a parrot'
got into the language.

'The Ghost' who was struck by lightning.
Johnny White.

3 Glory, glory!

The first 'Glory, glory' team was in 1960.
That's when Spurs won the Double,
both the Cup and the League.
Spurs were the first to do that,
and only three others
have done it since.

Danny Blanchflower was the captain.
He was also captain of Ireland.
Bobby Smith scored the goals,
but the star of the team was 'The Ghost'.
That was what the fans called Johnny White.
He could drift round the field,
and appear suddenly
where nobody was expecting him.

He was only young,
and was going to be
one of the great names of football,
when he was struck by lightning
and killed.

In 1961, Spurs signed a new striker for £99,999.
That was a record in those days.
The striker was Jimmy Greaves.
He became Spurs' best goal scorer ever,
and perhaps the best in the country.

He wasn't very big,
but was very quick,
and had perfect balance.
He could dart into the goal area,
steady himself, and shoot,
before the defenders knew he was there.

He scored the winning goals for Spurs
in the FA Cup
and the European Cup-winners Cup.
Spurs were the first British club
to win a big European competition.

The big goal scorer, 'Greavsie'.
Tottenham Hotspur v Manchester United,
FA Cup semi-final, 1962.

Jimmy Greaves played for England too.
Everyone hoped
that he would help win the World Cup in 1966.
He did play in a few games,
but he didn't play very well.
He was dropped for the final.

Nobody knew at the time
that he had been very ill.
In the next few years
he had other illnesses
that stopped him playing his best.

After he left football,
Jimmy Greaves wrote a book about himself
which explained why he had so many illnesses.
He was an alcoholic.

He showed a lot of courage,
and fought hard against it,
but it was a long, long fight.

When Jimmy Greaves
had beaten alcoholism,
he became a football presenter on television.
And now 'Greavsie'
is one of the most popular figures in football.

Another star was Cyril Knowles.
He is the only footballer
to have a hit record named after him.

A record producer was watching Spurs,
and he heard the fans sing this song.

> *Nice one Cyril,*
> *Nice one son –*
> *Nice one Cyril,*
> *Let's avver-nuvver-wun!*

He thought it was so good
he made a record of it,
and it got to number one!

Ricky Villa and Ossie Ardiles, 1981.

4 More stars

In 1978, Argentina won the World Cup.
They had two stars,
Ossie Ardiles and Ricky Villa.
Spurs bought them both.

That's just like Spurs.
No other club had foreign players.
Spurs started it.
But they didn't just have one,
they had two.
And they didn't just have any foreign player,
they had the two biggest stars in the world.

When Spurs do something,
they do it in a big way.

When they began playing for Spurs,
Ardiles and Villa didn't play very well.
It took time to get used to English football.
But when they had settled in,
Spurs began to play better and better.

In 1981, they won the Cup.
Ricky Villa scored the winning goal.
It was one of the best goals
ever seen at Wembley.
He started a long run,
round and round the defenders,
and then hit a hard, low shot into the goal.
Then he started a longer run,
round and round the ground,
dancing with joy!

Another star of this time was Glen Hoddle.
He was the cleverest player
and the best passer of his day.
He didn't score many goals,
but he could read the game,
and work out how to beat the other side.
Whether to play more on the left,
or on the right,
or to put more balls through the centre.

The fans called him,
'The King of White Hart Lane.'

When he stopped playing,
he became very religious.
He said he had found God.

One fan said,
'It must have been a great pass.'

The King of White Hart Lane.
Glenn Hoddle.

5 The biggest and the best

In 1982, Spurs opened a new stand.
But it wasn't just any stand.
One fan said it was a five star, luxury hotel
where you could,
if you wanted,
watch some football!
There were bars,
private dining rooms,
executive suites, and so on.

That's just like Spurs:
everything has to be the biggest and the best.
But the biggest and the best
is also the most expensive as well!

That stand nearly bankrupted Spurs,
and so in 1983
Tottenham Hotspur Football Club
became Tottenham Hotspur plc.

That's just like Spurs.

If other clubs get short of money,
they get a loan.
If Spurs get short of money,
they become a 'limited company'
and are 'floated on the Stock Exchange'
to raise money from 'Shareholders'.

The manager left.
He said that Spurs had become a business
not a football club.
But it did save Spurs,
and raise them a lot more money.

They soon spent it!

6 Gazza

In 1987, Terry Venables became manager.
He used to play for Spurs.
Then he was manager of Barcelona.
He had made them the top team in Europe.
The Spanish fans called him 'El Tel'.

He came to Spurs for a record sum of money,
and started to buy players
for more record sums.
He bought Paul Gascoigne for £2 million,
and Gary Lineker for £1.2 million.

Gazza soon became the fans' favourite.
He was just like Spurs,
brilliant one minute and daft the next.
After the World Cup in 1990,
when he cried on television,
he was said to be worth £15 million.

Gascoigne and Lineker celebrate
beating Arsenal 3–1.

During this time
Spurs were always in the news.
But it was never about football.
It was about money
and shares and big business.
There were two main business people,
Robert Maxwell and Alan Sugar.
They were both millionaires.
Robert Maxwell ran newspapers
like the *Daily Mirror*,
and Alan Sugar got his money from computers.

They both put a lot of money in Spurs.
In 1991 Robert Maxwell was found dead.
It was said to be an accident,
but no-one is really sure.
Robert Maxwell had stolen
huge sums of money
by doing crooked deals.
No-one knows exactly how much.

It was only discovered
after he was dead.

Maxwell's companies collapsed.
Suddenly Spurs were in real trouble.
It seemed for a time
that they would collapse as well.

And then Terry Venables and Alan Sugar
rescued Spurs.
They joined together and took over the club.
Alan Sugar became Chairman
and Terry Venables became
Chief Executive and manager.

For a time everything seemed right for Spurs,
but a row started between them,
and Terry Venables was sacked.
He took Alan Sugar to court.
Alan Sugar took Terry Venables to court.
And so it went on.

It still hasn't been sorted out.
Terry Venables became England coach,
and was doing really well.
But he decided to leave
to sort out all the legal rows.

Big business.
Alan Sugar and Terry Venables.

But while Spurs were making news off the field,
they were also doing great things on it.

They won the Cup in 1991
for a record eighth time.
Gazza had been brilliant
in the run-up to the Cup.
He had won the semi-final almost by himself.

Everyone was hoping
he would do the same in the Final.
But he went right over the top.
He was nearly sent off in the first few minutes,
and then he tried to slice a defender in half
with a crazy late tackle.
The other side scored from the free kick.
But, what was worse,
Gazza was still on the ground.
In that foul he had torn his knee.
He was carried off the field
and he'd hardly touched the ball.

Spurs fought back and won 2–1,
but it was Gazza's last game for Spurs.

7 The team today

When he was better after his injury,
Gazza left Spurs to play in Italy.
Someone asked him about the language.
'No problem,' said Gazza,
'I can't speak English yet!'

Gary Lineker also left Spurs,
to play in Japan.
But then in 1994,
one of the world's top stars joined Spurs.
Jorgen Klinsmann.

He was Germany's top goal scorer,
and had won the World Cup with them.
He had played all over the world.

Soon his blond hair and dashing style
made him a star with Spurs fans as well.
But he only stayed for one season.

Jurgen Klinsmann,
Germany's top goal scorer,
joins Tottenham Hotspur.

Darren Anderton and Teddy Sheringham
also joined Spurs.
They both play for England,
and Spurs fans are hoping
they can take Spurs to the top again.
Because that's where they ought to be.
The 'Glory, Glory' team,
the most exciting and stylish team
in the country.